C000109131

CORNERSTONES
for
Writing

Pupil's Book
Year 6

**Alison Green, Jill Hurlstone,
Diane Skipper and Jane Woods**

Series Editor
Jean Glasberg

CAMBRIDGE
UNIVERSITY PRESS

Five steps to

GOOD WRITING

1 **Modelling:** use a model text to help you learn how to write your own text

Use the activities in this book

2 **Plan your own text**

Use the planning frames or the activities in this book

3 **Draft your text**

Work on your own text

4 **Revise and edit your text**

Work on your own text

5 **Publish your text**

Work on your own text

When you see this symbol, do this activity with a partner or in a group.

CONTENTS

How to write

in the style of a classic story

1 Classic story style

1 Read this passage from *Treasure Island*.

Find an expression in the text that shows this is *not* a modern story.

Identify the things that Jim can see, hear and smell.

> There was not a breath of air moving, nor a sound but that of the surf booming half a mile away along the beaches and against the rocks outside. A peculiar stagnant smell hung over the anchorage – a smell of sodden leaves and rotting tree trunks. I observed the doctor sniffing and sniffing, like someone tasting a bad egg.
>
> "I don't know about treasure," he said, "but I'll stake my wig there's fever here."

From *Treasure Island* by R.L. Stevenson

How do you imagine Treasure Island?

Discuss your ideas with a partner, and together write three more things that Jim might see, hear and smell when he goes ashore.

4

2 Read this passage from *Treasure Island*.

In your book, write down all the words and phrases that show this is *not* a modern story.

Make a list of some of the things Jim can see and hear, and the adjectives the author uses to describe them. What impression do they give of the island?

Discuss your ideas with a partner. What else do you think Jim might see, hear and smell? What adjectives would help the reader to picture the scene?

Jim sets out to explore Treasure Island for the first time ...

I had crossed a marshy tract full of willows, bulrushes and odd, outlandish, swampy trees; and I had now come out upon the skirts of an open piece of undulating, sandy country, about a mile long, dotted with a few pines, and a great number of contorted trees, not unlike the oak in growth, but pale in the foliage, like willows. On the far side of the open stood one of the hills, with two quaint, craggy peaks, shining vividly in the sun.

I now felt for the first time the joy of exploration. The isle was uninhabited; my shipmates I had left behind, and nothing lived in front of me but dumb brutes and fowls. I turned hither and thither among the trees. Here and there were flowering plants, unknown to me; here and there I saw snakes, and one raised his head from a ledge of rock and hissed at me with a noise not unlike the spinning of a top. Little did I suppose that he was a deadly enemy, and that the noise was the famous rattle.

From Treasure Island by R.L. Stevenson

3 The next sentence from this passage begins like this:

"Then I came to …"

Copy these words into your book, and complete the narrator's description of what he saw in the style of R.L. Stevenson.

Use this list of old-fashioned words to help you.

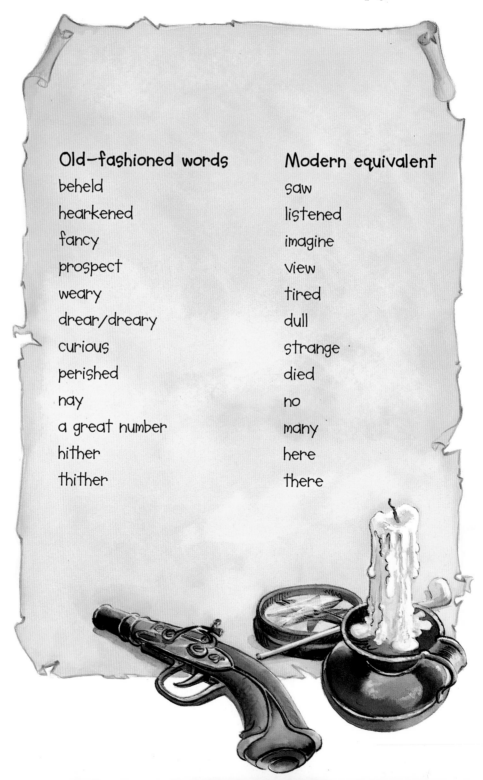

Old-fashioned words	Modern equivalent
beheld	saw
hearkened	listened
fancy	imagine
prospect	view
weary	tired
drear/dreary	dull
curious	strange
perished	died
nay	no
a great number	many
hither	here
thither	there

1 Write about what happens after Jim has been captured.

Use Long John Silver as the narrator.

Include a conversation between Jim and Silver.

Use the ideas box on page 8 and the 'piratespeak' vocabulary below to help you.

You can also use the old-fashioned vocabulary on page 6.

'Piratespeak'

Cap'n   Shiver my timbers!   Ay ay!   shipmate   Avast there!
By thunder!   shipshape   Yo ho ho and a bottle of rum!

2 Write about what happens after Jim has been captured.

First, use Jim as the narrator.

Then write a version with Long John Silver as the narrator. Include a conversation between Jim and Silver, and a piece of description.

Try to write in the style of R.L. Stevenson!

Use the ideas box below and the 'piratespeak' vocabulary on page 7 to help you.

You can also use the old-fashioned vocabulary on page 6.

Ideas

What might happen to Jim after he is captured by pirates?

- Perhaps he decides to join them?
- Perhaps they force him to join them?
- Maybe they make him 'walk the plank'!

Hint!

R.L. Stevenson's pirates do not use standard grammar in their sentences. For example, they say 'ain't' instead of 'isn't' and they often add 'a' as a prefix to words, such as 'a-doing' and 'a-going'.

1   Plan your own story based on *Treasure Island*.
Choose one of the ideas below, or think up your own.

> Jim hears an empty bottle clanking against the side of the ship and sees that it contains a slip of paper. He climbs down to retrieve it and finds a message from his mother, who has found an exciting new piece of information about the treasure ...
>
> After a terrible storm, the crew realise that the ship's rowing boat has been lost. In an effort to reach the island, both Jim and Silver secretly try to build their own craft using objects from around the ship ...
>
> The Hispaniola is moored one night in a lagoon where the water is especially clear. Jim notices what looks like a golden chest, hundreds of feet down on the sea floor, glinting in the moonlight. He knows that he couldn't reach it without the help of the whole crew, and has to decide what to do before dawn, when they have to set sail ...

When you have decided on your story, use **copymaster 2** to write the plan.

2   Plan your own story, based on *Treasure Island*.
Choose one of the ideas above, or think up your own.

ADDITIONAL SESSIONS

Writing a modern retelling of a classic story

1 This passage describes a scene between the captain and Black Dog. Read the passage.
Now rewrite it using a modern setting and up-to-date language.

"Now, look here," said the captain; "you've run me down; here I am; well, then, speak up: what is it?"

"That's you, Bill," returned Black Dog, "you're in the right of it, Billy. I'll have a glass of rum from this dear child here, as I've took such a liking to; and we'll sit down, if you please, and talk square, like old shipmates."

When I returned with the rum, they were already seated on either side of the captain's breakfast table – Black Dog next to the door, and sitting sideways, so as to have one eye on his old shipmate, and one, as I thought, on his retreat.

He bade me go, and leave the door wide open. "None of your keyholes for me, sonny," he said; and I left them together and retired into the bar.

From *Treasure Island* by R.L. Stevenson

2 The passages above and below describe what happens next between the captain and Black Dog.

Read both passages. Now rewrite the one below using a modern setting and up-to-date language.

Then all of a sudden there was a tremendous explosion of oaths and other noises – the chair and table went over in a lump, a clash of steel followed, and then a cry of pain, and the next instant I saw Black Dog in full flight, and the captain hotly pursuing, both with drawn cutlasses, and the former streaming blood from the left shoulder. Just at the door, that captain aimed at the fugitive one last tremendous cut, which would certainly have split him to the chine had it not been intercepted by our big signboard of Admiral Benbow. You may see the notch on the lower side of the frame to this day.

From Treasure Island by R.L. Stevenson

3 Look at the extracts from *Treasure Island* above, and the passage below. They describe what happens next between the captain and Black Dog.

Rewrite the passage below using a modern setting and up-to-date language.

"Jim," says he, "rum"; and as he spoke, he reeled a little and caught himself with one hand against the wall.
"Are you hurt?" cried I.
"Rum," he repeated. "I must get away from here. Rum! rum!"
I ran to fetch it; but I was quite unsteadied by all that had fallen out, and I broke one glass and fouled the tap, and while I was still getting in my own way, I heard a loud fall in the parlour, and, running in, beheld the captain lying full length upon the floor. At the same instant my mother, alarmed by the cries and fighting, came running downstairs to help me. Between us we raised his head. He was breathing very loud and hard; but his eyes were closed, and his face a horrible colour.
"Dear, deary me," cried my mother, "what a disgrace upon the house! And your poor father sick!"

From Treasure Island by R.L. Stevenson

Writing a story as a playscript

1   Write a scene for a play based on this passage from *Treasure Island*.

The scene is set in the village inn.

The characters are Jim, the captain and Black Dog.

Hint!

Set out your playscript with each new character on a new line.

2   Write a scene for a play based on this passage from *Treasure Island*.

First write a brief description of the setting in which the scene takes place. Then decide on the characters. What do they say to each other?

Hint!

Add stage directions – use brackets to separate them from the dialogue.

"Now, look here," said the captain; "you've run me down; here I am; well, then, speak up: what is it?"

"That's you, Bill," returned Black Dog, "you're in the right of it, Billy. I'll have a glass of rum from this dear child here, as I've took such a liking to; and we'll sit down, if you please, and talk square, like old shipmates."

When I returned with the rum, they were already seated on either side of the captain's breakfast table – Black Dog next to the door, and sitting sideways, so as to have one eye on his old shipmate, and one, as I thought, on his retreat.

He bade me go, and leave the door wide open. "None of your keyholes for me, sonny," he said; and I left them together and retired into the bar.

From *Treasure Island* by R.L. Stevenson

Writing a poem using active verbs and personification

1 You are going to write a poem about a volcano.

Here are some active verbs that could be used in your poem. Copy them into your book and think of four more.

> boiled   rushed   roared   tumbled

Use some of the verbs you have written down to finish this poem.

Now add some extra lines to the poem, using more of your verbs.

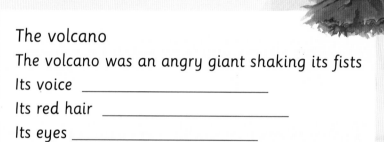

The volcano
The volcano was an angry giant shaking its fists
Its voice _____
Its red hair _____
Its eyes _____

2 Choose one of these subjects and make a list of active verbs that could be used to personify it:

- the sea
- rain
- winter
- the television
- the moon

Write a poem about your subject. Think of it as a person and describe its appearance.

Hint!

Your poem will be more effective if you give your subject a distinct character. For example, describing winter as a 'grumpy old man' will be more interesting than just describing it as 'a man'. Include some active verbs to help the thing seem more like a person. For example, you could describe winter as 'a grumpy old man stamping through the garden'.

3 When you have written a draft of your poem, read it through and edit it.

Use the following checklist to help you:

- Have you given your subject a distinct character?

- Have you used active verbs?

- Can you use different words to make your descriptions more interesting?

4 Read this poem.

Find examples of objects that are personified and list them in your book.

Find as many active verbs as you can and list these as well.

Who do you think the 'big bully' is?

Autumn Gale

A Dickens of a day! You can't tell leaves
from birds – panicky things
hurtling past windows. Everything's
having a rough time. Hedges shivering
with fright: that plastic bag
tugging to free itself from the barbs
of the blackthorn, this back-garden willow
taking such stick it's nearly thrashed
out of its wits. Some big bully
is terrorizing the neighbourhood,
huffing and puffing to blow your house down.

by Matt Simpson

2 How to write
a biographical recount

1 Recount structure

1 Read this orientation from a biography of Isambard Kingdom Brunel.

> Isambard Kingdom Brunel was a Victorian engineer who became famous for designing bridges, tunnels, ships and railways using methods not seen before. He worked all over Britain right up to his death in 1859.

Draw a table like this in your book.

Put all the facts in the 'Information' column.

In the second column, write what each fact tells you, using the words *who, what, where, when, why*.

The first fact has been done for you!

Information	What it tells me
Isambard Kingdom Brunel	<u>Who</u> he is

2 Choose a person you know well.

Note some key facts about them:
- who they are;
- their relationship to you;
- what they do;
- why they are special;
- where they live.

Now write the orientation for their biography.
Write only two or three sentences and keep to the key facts!

3 Read these orientations from three biographies.

J.K. Rowling's first Harry Potter novel was published in 1997. Since then her stories about the young apprentice wizard have sold millions of copies worldwide, making her a famous name in the book world.

Steven Spielberg has entertained many millions of people worldwide and is now considered to be the most successful film maker of all time.

William Shakespeare is a famous playwright. All over the world his plays are still being performed, more than 400 years after they were written.

For each orientation write out the facts in order of appearance.

Next to each fact write either *who*, *what*, *where*, *when* or *why*.

Is there any pattern in the order of facts? With a partner, discuss why you think this is.

1   Read the biography of Isambard
    Kingdom Brunel on **copymaster 3**.

    Identify and label the orientation, key events section and
    reorientation.
    Then draw a table like this in your book.
    Find words or phrases that show the passing of time between
    paragraphs in the key events section.
    Write them in the table.
    Next to each one write a different word or
    phrase that has a similar meaning.

Paragraph	Connective words/phrases	Alternative

2   Read the biography of Steven Spielberg on **copymaster 4**.
    Identify and label the orientation, key events section and
    reorientation.
    Then draw a table in your book like the one shown above.
    Write in words or phrases that link events together within any
    paragraph.
    Next to each one write a different word or phrase that has a
    similar meaning.

3 Read the biography of Steven Spielberg on **copymaster 4**.

Find and underline any time connectives.

Choose the paragraph with the most examples and rewrite it using different time connectives.

Remember to:

- keep the meaning the same;
- use the class 'Connectives' chart to help you;
- read your paragraph to a partner to check that it makes sense.

1 Read these quotations with a partner.

Show where you would place each quotation in the Brunel biography on **copymaster 3**.

Discuss what extra information each quotation gives you about Brunel.

"If great engineering consists in effecting huge monuments of madness at an enormous cost to shareholders, then this Mr Brunel is surely the greatest of all engineers."

(From *The Field* magazine)

"He was a man with the greatest originality of thought and power of execution, bold in his plans, but right."

(Friend and engineer, Daniel Gooch)

"We went down the shaft on the South Bank and got into a punt, which he was to steer into the tunnel. But Brunel, swinging carelessly from left to right, fell overboard and out went the candles."

(A co-worker on the Thames Tunnel)

2 Read these quotations with a partner.

Show where you would place each quotation in the Spielberg biography on **copymaster 4**.

Discuss what extra information each quotation gives you about Spielberg.

"Directing is 80 per cent communicating and 20 per cent know-how."

(Steven Spielberg, 1987)

"Spielberg has done the best directing of his career. Much of his previous work has been clever, but Schindler's List is masterly ... This may be the start of a new period in Spielberg's prodigious career – Part Two: The Man."

(S. Kauffman, *New Republic* magazine, 1993)

"For years he just scared us. Now he gets to scare the masses."

(Anne Spielberg, after seeing *Jaws* in 1975)

3 Read this reorientation from the Steven Spielberg biography:

> Spielberg is not without his critics. Some feel that his films lack artistic depth. No one, however, can deny his ability to control the emotions of his audience.

Now draw a table like this in your book.
Complete it for this reorientation.

Main aspect of life to be summed up	Evaluative comments made	The writer's opinion

Planning the biography

1 Decide which of the following questions are open.

Use these to help you write some open questions for your interview.

1 Did you enjoy your childhood?
2 Which was your most exciting invention?
3 What can you remember about your most dangerous job?
4 What can you tell me about your greatest achievement?
5 Did you have any ambitions as a child?
6 When was your happiest moment?
7 What would you tell your children if they wanted to become engineers?
8 If you had the chance to go back in time, what would you change about your life as an engineer?

2 Rewrite these questions for Steven Spielberg to encourage him to give you more information.

1 What was the first film to make an impression on you?

2 Did you know as a child what you wanted to do with your life?

3 When did you first become interested in making films?

4 What is the most difficult job you have to do when making a film?

5 Which of your films did you most enjoy making?

6 What is your favourite film?

7 Have your children shown any interest in going into the film world?

8 Do you have an idea for another film?

3 Improve these open questions by giving them a focus. Check your improvements by interviewing a partner. Rewrite the questions again if necessary.

1 What can you remember about your early childhood?

2 What do you think the future holds for you?

3 What do you have strong opinions about?

4 What do you feel people should do with their lives?

5 What do you feel needs to be changed in the world?

ADDITIONAL SESSIONS

Descriptions from different perspectives

1 Using **copymaster 6**, continue to write the school report for J.K. Rowling.

Use these extracts from her biography and autobiography to help you.

... at school, she continued to develop her skills when entertaining friends during lunch breaks with long serial stories in which they performed heroic and daring deeds.

I was quiet, freckly, short-sighted and rubbish at sports (I am the only person I know who managed to break their arm playing netball). My favourite subject by far was English, but I quite liked languages too.

I did once have a fight with the toughest girl in my year, but I didn't have a choice, she started hitting me and it was hit back or lie down and play dead. For a few days I was quite famous because she hadn't managed to flatten me. The truth was that my locker was right behind me and held me up. I spent weeks afterwards peering nervously around corners in case she was waiting to ambush me.

I wrote a lot in my teens, but I never showed any of it to my friends, except for funny stories that (again) featured us all in thinly disguised characters.

From *The Not Especially Fascinating Life So Far of J.K. Rowling*

2 Continue to write the personal letter about J.K. Rowling.
Use the extracts on page 24 to help you.

3 Continue to write the character reference for J.K. Rowling.
Use this extract to help you.

After studying French and Classics at University, she worked for five years as a secretary. "All I ever liked about working in offices was being able to type up stories on the computer when no one was looking," she recalls. It was on a train journey to London at this time that the idea for Harry Potter first came to her.

Writing in a journalistic style

1 Imagine you are a journalist.

Here are some notes about Brunel. Write them as a paragraph from a newspaper report.

Main message:

Brunel – one of Britain's greatest and most inventive engineers.

Supporting details:

* Designed and built famous/ingenious Clifton Suspension Bridge – still in use today.

* Built important railway line – from London to Bristol. Found best route.

* Designed/built giant steamships – made of iron – to speed up journey Britain to America.

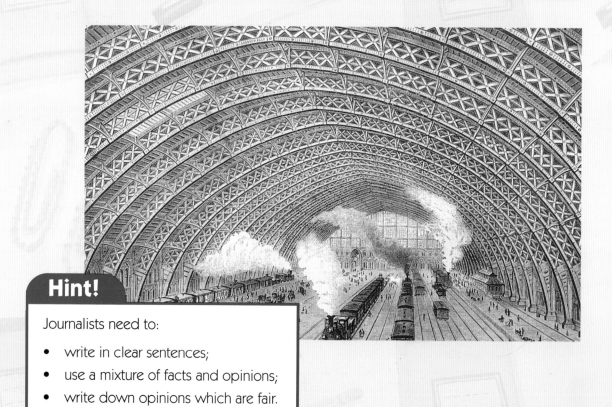

Hint!

Journalists need to:

* write in clear sentences;
* use a mixture of facts and opinions;
* write down opinions which are fair.

2 Read this newspaper report about Steven Spielberg.

Write out the **facts** in one colour and the **opinions** in a different colour.

Is there a good balance of facts and opinions?

Try to find an opinion that you think is not fair or misleads the reader.

If asked to think of a well-known and successful film director, many people would name Steven Spielberg. His internationally famous films, covering a wide variety of themes, have become household names and have appealed to viewers both young and old. What special qualities does this unique man have to hold millions of people enthralled by his films?

His intense interest in films began during his childhood and was to stay with him into adulthood. Determined to get into the professional film-making world, he used his powers of persuasion to convince the Hollywood producers Zanuck and Brown to let him direct the filming of a new novel, *Jaws*, the story of a great white killer shark. In 1973 they finally agreed.

The young and relatively inexperienced Spielberg had clear ideas from the start about how the novel should be made into a film. As filming proceeded, one of his many jobs included mastering the difficult controls of 'Bruce', the seven metre long mechanical shark. But with his technical skill and determination to succeed, he won through. The film opened in 1975 to instant success, breaking all existing box office records. At the age of 28, Spielberg had leapt to the forefront of the film world. He has never looked back.

3 Look at the biography of Steven Spielberg on **copymaster 4**.

Choose one paragraph and rewrite it in journalistic style.

Think about:

- the main message of the paragraph;
- how the first sentence can get this main message across;
- using simple sentence structure;
- how to keep the reader's interest.

Writing a newspaper report

1 Rewrite these headlines about Brunel in a more sensational style.

SUCCESSFUL BRIDGING OF RIVER AVON

FIRE BREAKS OUT ON WOODEN STEAMSHIP

BRUNEL
IN DANGER AS
SHIP BURNS

QUEEN VICTORIA: FIRST MONARCH TO TRAVEL BY TRAIN

SAFELY LAUNCHED – WORLD'S FIRST IRON SHIP

Hint!

Sensational writing tries to:

- exaggerate the message;
- stir up the reader's feelings.

2 Here is part of a newspaper report about Steven Spielberg. Rewrite it in a more sensational style.

Steven Spielberg, a new name in the film world, was yesterday swept overboard from a small boat when filming in the treacherous waters off the coast of Massachusetts.

The director and his crew were filming a scene involving a man-eating shark for his next film, *Jaws*, when a freak wave hit the boat. The boat was thrown off course causing Spielberg to lose his balance. He was tossed into the water where he quickly became lost from view in the swirling currents. This stretch of water is notoriously dangerous and the crew feared for his life.

3 Read the biography of Steven Spielberg on **copymaster** 4.

Pick out an interesting event.

Write a paragraph about it for a newspaper report in standard English.

Then write a paragraph about the same event in a sensational style.

3 How to write

a mystery story with flashbacks

1 What makes a detective mystery?

1 Read the review of *The Mystery of the Missing Painting*. What are the key features of a detective mystery like this? Copy the table on page 31. List the key features on the chart.

The Mystery of the Missing Painting

The story starts with the discovery that a painting has been stolen from an art gallery in Manchester. The security guard, David Robinson, starts work at 8 a.m. on Tuesday morning and finds that the painting has been cut from its frame. Detective Romas Bates is called and finds a knife and a ring on the floor. He notices that a small window was left open – this may have been the thief's escape route. He finds out that Heather Brierley, an artist, had visited the gallery the day before. She told her friend that she wanted the painting that has now been stolen – to hang in her house. Romas Bates also discovers that the security guard needs extra money to pay for a new sports car. The detective then finds a tiny thread of material, from the security guard's uniform, caught on the picture frame. This solves the mystery. It was the security guard who stole the painting and used the security code to escape through the door. The window had been left open by mistake. Heather Brierley's ring had slipped off her finger during her visit to the art gallery the day before.

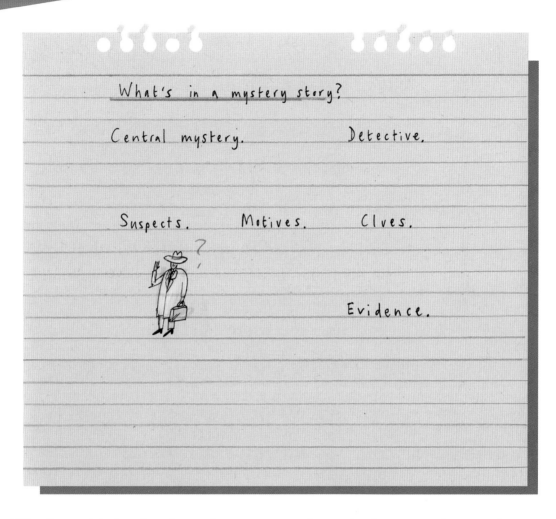

What's in a mystery story?

Central mystery.   Detective.

Suspects.   Motives.   Clues.

                                    Evidence.

2 Think of a detective mystery that you have read recently.
What are the key features of a detective story?

Copy the table above, adding three more boxes as follows:

Witness(es)
Alibi(s)
Red herring(s)

List the key features on the table.

1 Write another diary entry for Benjamin Fisher. Use the following as your opening lines:

> Jake inched closer. "Keep reading."
> "June 20th 8.30 p.m. ...

2 Read this extract from *Truth or Dare* by Celia Rees.

Write the next chapter, including a flashback, using one of the techniques you have learnt.

Try to change the setting in your flashback.

The story so far:

Josh is 13 years old. It is the summer holidays and Josh and his mother, Joanna, have gone to stay with Josh's grandmother because she is ill. Josh knows that his mother had a brother, Patrick, who supposedly died of pneumonia when he was 13. As he settles into his room at the top of the house, Josh feels that there is something mysterious about his uncle. Then he finds a small door cut into the wall ...

It was cut into the painted wooden panelling and led into a crawl-way between the roof and the eaves. Josh wriggled his head and shoulders in, but it was too dark to see anything. He groped his way along, his eyes adjusting to the faint light filtering through the slates. There was something shoved up at the far end. It looked like a box or a case.

Josh worked his way along the gap. He'd grown a lot lately, filling out, getting broader across the shoulders. It was a tight fit. Claustrophobia grabbed at him briefly, squeezing the space around him. He tried to ignore the nagging fear of being trapped forever and used his elbows, knees and feet to pull and push himself until he could reach forward and touch the object.

It was a flat lidded box. He hooked a finger under the edge and pulled it with him, inching backwards into the room again. It was a suitcase. A small leather one. Through the dust he could see the initials P.A.J. stamped in black in the bottom corner. The P could stand for Paul, but the A stood for Alan, Joshua knew. It was his middle name too, so the original owner of this case must have been Patrick Alan Jordan.

Josh left the rest of the cleaning, the bed-making, everything, to concentrate on his find. He sat cross-legged on the floor before it and carefully wiped the top. The catches on either side of the handle were not locked. Josh slid them sideways, triggering the hasps and flipping up the lid ...

From Truth or Dare by Celia Rees

3 A diamond necklace has been stolen from Linda Harris during a power cut at a party in Greenbank Mansions.

There were five people in the room when the lights went out, and the same five were there when the lights came back on.

Detective Rowlands has come to question the suspects about what happened when the lights went out.

Name:	**BEN HARIFA**
Age:	30
Occupation:	Party organiser
Motive:	Needs money to pay business bills.

Name:	**MATTHEW WRIGHT**
Age:	25
Occupation:	Racehorse owner
Motive:	Needs money to buy new racehorse.

Name:	**LINDA HARRIS**
Age:	35
Occupation:	Jewellery dealer
Motive:	Owner of the necklace. Has a client who will pay her £1 million for it.

Name:	**JEANETTE HARRIS**
Age:	41
Occupation:	Banker
Motive:	Linda Harris's sister. Believes that the necklace, which belonged to their mother, should be hers.

Name:	**SAFIA PATEL**
Age:	26
Occupation:	Beauty consultant
Motive:	Wants diamond necklace, but can't afford one.

Name:	**MARIA ROWLANDS**
Age:	28
Occupation:	Detective Chief Inspector

Work as a group. One person is the detective, and the others are suspects.

First, the detective leaves the group while the suspects decide who the thief is.

Then the detective returns and asks each suspect for a flashback account of what they were doing when the necklace went missing.

Next, the detective questions each suspect.

Finally, the detective identifies the thief.

1 Imagine that you are the person in the picture. You are walking through the dark woods when you find a mysterious suitcase.

Read the account below and copy it into your book.

Fill in the gaps with words that will make your adventure sound more mysterious. Use the class word bank and the word box to help you.

I was walking home through the _____ woods when it started to rain. The wind _____ through the trees and the branches _____ . I heard some twigs _____ and I turned around, but no one was there. I started to shiver and _____ ahead of me to see if I could see the end of the path. Suddenly, my foot hit something hard. I _____ down to see a _____ suitcase on the ground, under the tree. I _____ picked it up and _____ out of the woods.

Word box
cautiously
shuddered
eerie
crouched
strange
crackled
creaking
whistled
battered
stared
snap
crept
sneaked

Can you use new words to make your story even more mysterious?

Compare your story to your partner's. Whose is more mysterious? Why?

2   Read the next part of the story that you began in the shared session.

What do you think lies behind the door? Describe the scene to your partner, using interesting 'mystery vocabulary'.

Use the class word bank and the word box on page 36.

> Another brilliant flare of light ripped open the sky, and flooded the tower room with incandescent silver.
>
> They all looked paler in the dark that followed. But Colin was pointing at the wall, just behind Claudia's head.
>
> "Look!"
>
> Everyone turned.
>
> "What?"
>
> "I can't see anything."
>
> "What's the matter?"
>
> "Look!" Colin said again. "In the wall. It's a door. There's a door hidden in the wall."

From Step by Wicked Step by Anne Fine

Now write the next paragraph of the story, trying to make the atmosphere as mysterious as possible.

3   Imagine that you are part of the crew on this boat. Strange sounds have been heard and one of the crew is missing.

Tell your partner what you think is happening.

Finally, write a description of the atmosphere on the boat.

Planning the mystery

1 Imagine that one of your friends witnessed these events on the way to school one day. They decide to try and solve the mystery of what happened.

Use **copymaster 9** to plan your own detective mystery.

Now tell your partner about your plot plan.

2 Use **copymaster 9** and this blurb from a book to plan your own detective mystery.

> When Annie and Joe arrive on the tropical island of Exotiki, they find themselves hurled into a sinister conspiracy. Their friend Polly has mysteriously disappeared leaving a hastily scrawled message which sets them on a breathless trail of investigation. Soon they are heading into the Exotikan jungle in search of the secrets of an ancient civilisation and a fabulous emerald with strange and mystic powers.

Now describe your plot plan to your partner.

3 Choose the headline, the postcard or the poster. Use **copymaster 10** to plan your own detective mystery.

Describe your plot plan to your partner.

ADDITIONAL SESSION

How to write a parody of a classic poem

'The Charge of the Mouse Brigade' (below) is a parody of
'The Charge of the Light Brigade'.

Half an inch, half an inch,
Half an inch onward,
Into Cat Valley
Rode the Six Hundred.
"Forward the Mouse Brigade!
Ravage their fleas!" he said.
"Capture the cheese!" he said.

From 'The Charge of the Mouse Brigade' by Bernard Stone

1 Write another verse for 'The Charge of the Mouse Brigade'.

Base it on this verse from 'The Charge of the Light Brigade'.
Use the framework on **copymaster 12** to help you.

Cannon to right of them,
Cannon to left of them,
Cannon in front of them
Volley'd and thunder'd;
Storm'd at with shot and shell,
Boldly they rode and well,
Into the jaws of Death,
Into the mouth of Hell
Rode the six hundred.

From 'The Charge of the Light Brigade' by Alfred, Lord Tennyson

2 Look at the parody 'The Charge of the Mouse Brigade' on page 40.

Use this verse from the original poem to help you continue the parody, using your own ideas.

Flash'd all their sabres bare,
Flash'd as they turn'd in air
Sabring the gunners there,
Charging an army, while
All the world wonder'd:
Plunged in the battery-smoke
Right thro' the line they broke;
Cossack and Russian
Reel'd from the sabre-stroke
Shatter'd and sunder'd.
Then they rode back, but not
Not the six hundred.

From 'The Charge of the Light Brigade' by Alfred, Lord Tennyson

3 Look at the parody 'The Charge of the Mouse Brigade' on page 40.

Use both extracts from 'The Charge of the Light Brigade' on page 40 and on this page to help you continue the parody, using your own ideas.

4 How to write
a balanced report

1 How to organise a balanced report

1 Use **copymaster 13**.

2 Here is the introduction to a balanced report on fox hunting:

> Should fox hunting be banned? Animal rights groups believe that fox hunting is a cruel sport that causes unnecessary suffering to foxes. However, hunt supporters believe that fox hunting is a traditional sport, which controls the fox population.

Look at **copymaster 14**. Can you order the arguments into four paragraphs?

Copy the following framework into your book and write the letters 'for' and 'against' each argument in a sensible order.

Paragraph	Argument 'for' hunting	Argument 'against' hunting
1		
2		
3		
4		

Now write your own conclusion.

State which arguments you think are the strongest and weakest on each side.

Hint!

Write each argument and its counter-argument in the same paragraph.

3 Read this report about fox hunting. It is supposed to be balanced but the author has not included the points and evidence *against* fox hunting.

Rewrite the text as a balanced report, using the information in the box to help you.

Finally, write an opening summary and a conclusion.

- A maximum of 700 full time jobs will be lost if fox hunting is banned.

- Foxes suffer long and painful deaths when attacked by hounds.

- Hunting does not control the fox population. It would be more effective and humane to shoot foxes that steal livestock.

- Drag hunting involves hounds chasing a scent, but does not involve killing animals.

Hunt supporters believe that foxes are pests and need to be hunted to be controlled. Farmers often call in the hunt to track down a fox that has been killing livestock.

Pro-hunters think that fox hunting is not cruel as the fox dies very quickly when the hounds catch it.

A report by the Countryside Alliance states that there are 15,900 people whose jobs directly depend on fox hunting. Consequently, if hunting is banned, all these people will be out of work. This will cause great hardship and distress to many families.

Finally, fox hunting has been a traditional sport in Britain for 200 years. Hunters think that if it is made illegal, a part of British culture will be lost for ever.

1 Here are some sentences from a balanced report about dolphins. Copy the sentences into your book and complete them using one of the connectives in the word bank below.

1 Tuna fish live in the same waters as dolphins. _____ fishermen catch dolphins in their nets too.

2 No one knows how many dolphins die _____ many of them are hurt and die away from the net _____ they cannot be counted.

3 Environmentalists think that dolphins die a painful death _____ fishermen believe that they die quickly.

4 Fishermen are worried about using other methods of fishing because they think that many other sea creatures will die. _____ environmentalists are also concerned about this, they still want all nets which catch dolphins to be banned.

> **Connectives**
> although   because   but   however   so   therefore   whereas

Work with your group to find other connectives in different texts. Make a chart for the class. Alternatively, write some sentences of your own, using the connectives listed above.

2 Use **copymaster 15**.

Then write a final paragraph which discusses the strengths and weaknesses of each point of view.

3 Read the introduction and the arguments in the tuna debate.

Write a balanced account of the arguments to form the middle section of the report.

Then write a final paragraph which discusses the strengths and weaknesses of each view.

Tuna fish live in the same waters as dolphins. Consequently, fishermen catch dolphins in their nets when they are fishing for tuna. Laws have been passed to limit the number of dolphins that die in this way, but certain environmentalists believe that no dolphins should die as a result of tuna fishing. However, tuna fishermen think that a certain number of dolphin deaths is acceptable.

Environmentalists	Tuna fishermen
1. Point Catching dolphins in fishing nets will eventually endanger the species. Evidence No accurate statistics on how many dolphins die – many are injured and die away from the net. Their bodies are not counted.	1. Point Dolphins are <u>not</u> an endangered species. Evidence Dolphin population is stable. 3,000 per year can be killed without endangering the species.
2. Point Dolphins are intelligent creatures. They suffer long, slow deaths when caught in nets – unnecessary cruelty. Evidence Distressed calling to other dolphins. Observation by environmentalists.	2. Point Dolphins die quickly when they are caught in nets and many escape. Evidence New nets help dolphins escape. Dolphins in distress are shot.
3. Point All nets which catch dolphins should be banned and other forms of fishing introduced. Evidence Can use hook and line fishing or electronic sounds to locate tuna. This does not affect dolphins.	3. Point Number of nets which catch dolphins has been reduced – different fishing methods are now used. These are endangering other sea creatures. Evidence Twenty times as many other sea creatures (including sharks and turtles) are dying because of alternative tuna fishing methods. This is upsetting the whole ecosystem.

1 You are going to prepare an argument against homework.

Read this evidence.

Evidence

1 Children are tired at the end of a school day and need to spend their spare time doing other activities such as sport and music, and having time to play.

2 Parents force children to do their homework.

3 Research carried out by Durham University shows that children who did more than ten minutes of homework every night do not score higher on tests.

Use **copymaster 16**. Write in evidence to support each point.

Use your own research to add an argument of your own.

Summarise your case at the end and state what action you think should be taken.

Now present your case to the group.

2 Read this information.

Points 'for' homework

1 Homework develops skills which children will need when they become adults.

2 Children who do homework get better exam results.

3 Homework improves the relationship between parents and children.

Evidence 'for' homework

1 Homework teaches children to have self-discipline, work independently and meet deadlines. These are valuable skills needed in adult life.

2 Research carried out by OFSTED shows that children who regularly complete their homework get better exam results.

3 Parents are interested in what their children are learning about in school and they spend time together talking, rather than watching television.

Points 'against' homework

1 Children do not perform better at school as a result of doing homework.

2 Homework causes arguments between parents and children.

3 Too much homework can badly affect children's social skills.

Evidence 'against' homework

1 Parents force children to do their homework.

2 Children do not have time to play and socialise with other children. Therefore, they grow up lacking important social skills.

3 Research carried out by Durham University shows that children who do more than ten minutes of homework every night do not score higher on tests.

Hint!

- State your position clearly at the beginning.

- Present your strongest arguments first.

- Summarise your case at the end and state what action you think should be taken.

- Think about possible objections to your arguments.

Use **copymaster 16** to construct your argument 'for' or 'against' homework.

Write an opening statement to describe your position.

Decide on an order for the points. Write them in with the evidence that supports them.

Add a further point with supporting evidence from your own research.

Write a summary and say what action you think should be taken.

Now present your case to the group.

3 Can you think of possible objections to your arguments? How might you counter them in a debate?

Now present your case to the group.

ADDITIONAL SESSION

Using 'official' language

1 Your class is going to stay at an outdoor centre for a week.

You will be travelling by coach, staying in a hostel and doing lots of activities such as climbing, canoeing and horse riding.

The total cost is £55.

Your parents/guardians must fill in a booking form before you can go.

Design the booking form for your trip.

Hint!

- Make the layout of the form clear.
- Check that you have included all the necessary information.
- Use 'official' language.

Now swap forms with your partner. Fill out each other's forms. Are they clear and easy to complete?

2 Rewrite these signs in everyday language.

NO PEDESTRIANS

PUBLIC
CONVENIENCE

WE APOLOGISE FOR
ANY INCONVENIENCE
CAUSED DURING
THESE WORKS

CAUTION
WORK IN
PROGRESS!

THE CONSUMPTION
OF FOOD & DRINK
IS FORBIDDEN IN
THIS AREA

NO
EXIT

LIFT
OUT
OF ORDER

CYCLING PROHIBITED

5 How to write
a book review

Identifying the key features of a book review

1 Here is the introduction from a book review of *Harry Potter and the Goblet of Fire*. Read it carefully.

"What do they want photos for, Colin?"
"The Daily Prophet, I think!"
"Great," said Harry dully. "Exactly what I need. More publicity."

But like it or not, the "most famous boy in the world" gets plenty of publicity as he enters his fourth year at Hogwarts School of Witchcraft and Wizardry.

Once returned to Hogwarts after his summer holiday with the dreadful Dursleys and an extraordinary outing to the Quidditch World Cup, the 14-year-old Harry and his fellow pupils are enraptured by the promise of the Triwizard Tournament: an ancient, ritualistic tournament that brings Hogwarts together with two other schools of wizardry – Durmstrang and Beauxbatons – in heated competition. But when Harry's name is pulled from the Goblet of Fire, and he is chosen to champion Hogwarts in the tournament, the trouble really begins. Still reeling from the effects of a terrifying nightmare that has left him shaken, and with the lightning-shaped scar on his head throbbing with pain (a sure sign that the evil Voldemort, Harry's sworn enemy, is close), Harry at once becomes the most popular boy in school. Yet, despite his fame, he is totally unprepared for the furore that follows.

Now copy this framework into your book.

Under each heading, list the details you find in the introduction.

Try to list them in the order in which they appear in the text.

Characters	
Names:	Descriptions:
Setting	
Place:	
Time of year/season:	
Plot The main situation/problem: Key event 1: Key event 2: Key event 3: Hints of events to come: Other important details (e.g. key objects named):	

2 Here is the commentary section from the same review.

Identify the negative and positive comments.

Do you think, on balance, that the reviewer would recommend the book to readers of your age?

Harry Potter and the Goblet of Fire is the long-awaited, heavily hyped fourth instalment of a phenomenally successful series that has captured the imagination of millions of readers, young and old, across the globe. In this book, the teenage Harry has a certain gawky charm that fits well with his advancing adolescence. As the story moves on, Harry too moves on to a new level of maturity that leaves the reader wondering how he will learn from his experiences, and liking him all the more as a character.

This is a hefty volume: 636 pages, of which probably at least 200 could have been cut without detracting from the story. The weight and complexity of the book is perhaps a hint that Rowling now has her eye sharply focused on her adult audience, and the average young reader may well find its girth daunting. Rowling's ironic and pointed observations on tabloid journalism and the nature of media hype is just one of the references littered through the book that will tickle the grown-ups but may well fly over the heads of her young fans.

3 Write the concluding paragraph of this review.

On the basis of the rest of the review, do you think the writer will recommend the book?

Note any weaknesses under an appropriate sub-heading.

Hint!

Include in your recommendation:
- the target readership (e.g. 'for readers aged 10+');
- the genre of the book.

Try to sum up the appeal of the book with phrases like 'gripping from start to finish', 'spellbinding'.

Comment on the most important or strongest aspect of the book first, then look at other aspects in order of importance.

1 Draw up a planning framework for your own book review.

Copy these headings and make notes under each of them.

>**Introduction**
>
>**Commentary** (leave plenty of space beneath this heading!)
>
>**Recommendation**

Here are some questions to help you to consider the three main aspects you should include.

Characters

- Were the characters convincing? Did they seem 'real' to you?
- Does the author mainly use dialogue to convey what the characters are like?
- Are there good descriptions of the characters?
- Are there key moments (things the character says or does) that display their personality clearly?

Setting

- Where is the story set?
- Are these places described in some detail or only briefly? Do you have a clear picture of them?
- How important are they to the book (how do they affect the characters/the plot)?

Plot

- What is the main situation/problem?
- What are the key events? Are they all believable? Are they well described?
- What is the ending like? Is it convincing? Is it disappointing in any way?
- Is the plot fast-moving, or slow? What do you think are the most exciting/funny/sad moments?

Keeping a reading journal

1 Complete the reading journal framework on **copymaster 18** for a book you are reading.

2 Make your own reading journal.
Answer these questions about a book you are reading.
You can also add any other thoughts you may have!

Title:

Author:

Why did you choose this book?

Have you read/heard anything about it?

Have you read any other books by this author?

Why did the cover/blurb attract you?

After you have read the first chapter

Describe the main characters. Say what you like/dislike about them.

When and where is the story set? List some words and phrases which create atmosphere.

What is the main event/problem? What do you think will happen?

When you have read half of the book

Have you learnt any more about the characters? Do you still feel the same about them?

Is the plot interesting? What part do you think is the most exciting so far? List some words which build tension/suspense.

Can you predict how the book is going to end?

When you have finished the book

Did the story end as you expected? Why/why not?

How did the ending make you feel?

Did the characters change as the story progressed? How?

Did you like the author's style? Why/why not?

Evaluation

What are the strengths of the book, in your opinion?

Does it have any weak points? Show what changes you would make to improve the book.

Would you recommend this book?

Who do you think might enjoy it? (e.g. type/age of reader)

How to write a book blurb

1 Read this blurb for *South by South East* by Anthony Horowitz.

What does it tell you about the book? Note down all the information given.

> McGuffin had finished talking. The telephone was dead and any minute now he'd be joining it. The stuff he had spilled down the coat was blood, his own blood ...
>
> Tim Diamond, the world's worst private detective, is broke – as his smart-mouthed younger brother Nick is quick to remind him. So, when a mysterious stranger offers Tim a wodge of money for his overcoat, it seems like a stroke of good fortune. But there are worse things in life than being broke. Being pumped full of lead for one – which is what happens to the stranger and could soon be the fate of the Diamond brothers themselves, unless they can outwit the unknown assassin on their tail. Follow their thrilling adventures in this action-packed, fun-filled yarn!

From The Illustrated Mum by Jacqueline Wilson

> Star used to love Marigold, love me, love our life together. We three were the colourful ones, like the glowing pictures inked all over Marigold ...
>
> Covered from head to foot with glorious tattoos, Marigold is the brightest, most beautiful mother in the world. That's what Dolphin thinks (she just wishes her beautiful mum wouldn't stay out partying all night or go weird now and then). Her older sister, Star, isn't so sure any more. She loves Marigold too, but sometimes she just can't help wishing she were more *normal* ...
>
> A powerful and memorable tale for older readers.
>
> "Powerfully portrayed, sometimes shocking but ultimately uplifting."
> *The Bookseller*
>
> "Has all the qualities of her previous successes ... disturbingly perceptive and provocative."
> *The Guardian*
>
> SHORTLISTED FOR THE WHITBREAD AWARD

2 Read the blurbs above (for *South by South East* by Anthony Horowitz) and left (for *The Illustrated Mum* by Jacqueline Wilson).

Note down all the information given in each.

Consider these questions about the blurb:

What sort of events might turn out to be 'disturbing' or 'shocking'?

Why might teachers and parents want children to read stories that shock or disturb?

3 Read the blurb on page 56 (for *The Illustrated Mum* by Jacqueline Wilson) and the blurb below (for *Harry Potter and the Prisoner of Azkaban* by J.K. Rowling).

Note down all the information given in each.

Harry Potter, along with his best friends Ron and Hermione, is about to start his third year at Hogwarts School of Witchcraft and Wizardry. Harry can't wait to get back to school after the summer holidays. (Who wouldn't if they lived with the horrible Dursleys?) But when Harry gets to Hogwarts, the atmosphere is tense. There's an escaped mass murderer on the loose, and the sinister prison guards of Azkaban have been called in to guard the school ...

A fantastic new story featuring Harry and his friends from the spellbinding J.K. Rowling.

"The most eagerly awaited children's book for years."
The Evening Standard

"Spellbinding, enchanting, bewitching stuff."
The Mirror

"The Harry Potter books are that rare thing, a series of stories adored by parents and children alike."
The Daily Telegraph

From *Harry Potter and the Prisoner of Azkaban* by J.K. Rowling

Read the other blurb on page 56.
Which one makes you really want to read the book?

4 Here are some hints to help you with your own blurb writing.

Text extract

- Keep it short.
- Must be interesting and dramatic.
- Could be dialogue.
- Must give a 'flavour' of what the writing is like.

Synopsis

- Give key details about character, plot and setting, but don't give too much away!
- Start with a dramatic opening statement or intriguing question.
- Use lots of exciting words and dramatic phrases.
- End with a hint of what might happen next – consider using ellipsis (...) or a question.

Recommendation

- Keep it short.
- Sum up the book's main qualities persuasively.
- Use positive adjectives (e.g. 'magical', 'hilarious', 'enthralling').
- Give the target readership age.

Review quotes

- You could make some of these up for your blurb!
- Praise the book's qualities so that adults (teachers, librarians, parents) would be impressed enough to buy the book.

Annotating a passage of text

1   Read this extract about Harry Potter's first Quidditch lesson.

On **copymaster 19**, underline the words or phrases that the author uses to make it seem like a truly magical game for witches and wizards.

Wood reached into the crate and took out the fourth and last ball. Compared with the Quaffle and the Bludgers, it was tiny, about the size of a large walnut. It was bright gold and had little fluttering silver wings.

"*This*," said Wood, "is the Golden Snitch, and it's the most important ball of the lot. It's very hard to catch because it's so fast and difficult to see. It's the Seeker's job to catch it. You got to weave in and out of the Chasers, Beaters, Bludgers and Quaffle to get it before the other team's Seeker, because whichever Seeker catches the Snitch wins his team an extra hundred and fifty points, so they nearly always win. That's why Seekers get fouled so much. A game of Quidditch only ends when the Snitch is caught, so it can go on for ages – I think the record is three months, they had to keep bringing on substitutes so the players could get some sleep."

From *Harry Potter and the Philosopher's Stone* by J.K. Rowling

2 Read the extract below. It describes the very strange moment when Harry finds a magic train in the middle of a busy 'Muggle' station.

On **copymaster 20**, underline the words and phrases the author uses to create an exciting mix of ordinary and magical images.

How do the images affect the reader?

A scarlet steam engine was waiting next to a platform packed with people. A sign overhead said *Hogwarts Express, 11 o'clock.* Harry looked behind him and saw a wrought-iron archway where the ticket box had been, with the words *Platform Nine and Three-Quarters* on it. He had done it.

Smoke from the engine drifted over the heads of the chattering crowd, while cats of every colour wound here and there between their legs. Owls hooted to each other in a disgruntled sort of way over the babble and the scraping of heavy trunks. The first few carriages were already packed with students, some hanging out of the window to talk to their families, some fighting over seats. Harry pushed his trolley off down the platform in search of an empty seat. He passed a round-faced boy who was saying, "Gran, I've lost my toad again."

From Harry Potter and the Philosopher's Stone by J.K. Rowling

3 Read the extract below. It describes the first time that Harry meets Hagrid, who will soon become his very good friend.

Working on **copymaster 21**, use coloured pens to highlight the words and images that the author uses to keep readers on the edge of their seats. Why do these images work so well?

Can you find the place where the feeling of the piece changes abruptly? Try to work out how the author makes this happen.

BOOM.

The whole shack shivered and Harry sat bolt upright, staring at the door. Someone was outside, knocking to come in.

BOOM. They knocked again. Dudley jerked awake.

"Where's the cannon?" he said stupidly.

There was a crash behind them and Uncle Vernon came skidding into the room. He was holding a rifle in his hands – now they knew what had been in the long, thin package he had brought with them.

"Who's there?" he shouted. "I warn you – I'm armed!"

There was a pause. Then –

SMASH!

The door was hit with such force that it swung clean off its hinges and with a deafening crash landed flat on the floor.

A giant of a man was standing in the doorway. His face was almost completely hidden by a long, shaggy mane of hair and a wild, tangled beard, but you could make out his eyes, glinting like black beetles under all the hair.

The giant squeezed his way into the hut, stooping so that his head just brushed the ceiling. He bent down, picked up the door and fitted it easily back into its frame. The noise of the storm outside dropped a little. He turned to look at them all.

"Couldn't make us a cup o' tea, could yeh? It's not been an easy journey ..."

From *Harry Potter and the Philosopher's Stone* by J.K. Rowling

6 How to write

1 Structure and language

1 Read the following text.

List the key features of a non-chronological report. Note down examples from the text.

Then identify the 'explanation' section. Which language features helped you identify it?

Microbes

Human hands (even apparently clean ones) can carry unwanted, invisible passengers. Microbes! These micro-organisms exist naturally everywhere: in the air, in water, in materials and on skin.

What is a microbe?
All living things are made from very tiny cells. The smallest living things are made from just one cell. They are called micro-organisms, or microbes, because they are so small that they can only be seen using a microscope. There are three main types:

- viruses (from the Latin word meaning 'poison');
- bacteria;
- fungi.

How do 'coughs and sneezes spread diseases'?
Colds are caused by viruses which are transmitted via moisture droplets in a person's breath. Therefore, when someone with a cold breathes out (or coughs or sneezes), the cold viruses that enter the air can be inhaled by other people. If a person is infected, they will only recover when their immune system overpowers the invading microbes.

---

2 Read the following text about microbes in food.

Use the information from both this text and the one on page 62 to write a short explanation of why it is important to wash your hands before touching food.

Microbes in food

There are two main types of micro-organism that can attack your food – bacteria and fungi (or moulds). Some moulds are very obvious, for example, the white fluffy mould that grows on jam. Most bacteria, however, cannot be seen or tasted.

Microbes feed, grow and multiply very rapidly in food. If swallowed, they can cause illness in two different ways:

- Moulds and bacteria can cause stomach upsets.
- Some microbes excrete deadly toxins into food as they feed and grow. This causes food poisoning, which can be very serious.

 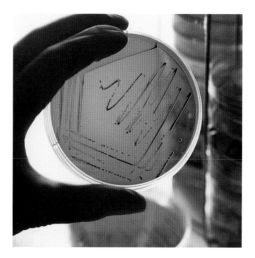

3 Build a glossary of technical vocabulary and other key words from the texts above.

1 Read the first section of the fire safety instructions below.

Using an acetate sheet, mark where explanations are given.

Then read the second section.

Write some short explanations to add to these instructions that will help the reader understand why they are important.

1 RAISE THE ALARM

If your smoke alarm goes off while you're asleep, don't investigate to see if there's a fire. Shout to wake everyone up. Get everyone together, follow your planned escape route and leave the building without running.

Check doors with the back of your hand. If they are warm, then the fire is on the other side, so do not open them.

If there is a lot of smoke, crawl along with your nose near the floor. Smoke rises, therefore the air will be cleaner near the floor.

2 ESCAPING FROM A WINDOW

If you are on the ground floor or first floor, you may be able to escape from a window. If you have to break the window, cover the jagged glass with towels or thick bedding.

Throw some more bedding out of the window to break your fall. Don't jump out of the window. Instead, lower yourself down to arm's length and drop to the ground.

If you have any very young children or elderly or disabled people with you, plan the order in which you will escape.

2 Read the following guidance about what to do if your escape route is blocked.

Copy out the instructions, and try to add explanations so that people can understand the reasons for them.

Get everyone into one room and close the door.

Put bedding or towels along the bottom of the door.

Open the window and stay near it.

Phone the Fire Brigade or shout for help.

Hint!

Here are some extra facts to help you:

- Smoke and fumes can kill people quickly.
- The firefighters need to know where you are.

3 Write a series of instructions about what to do if there is a fire at school.

If you can, base these on your school's existing fire safety rules.

Include explanations that give the reasons for your instructions.

1 Read this extract from a science journal kept by a pupil.

It is quite effective in recording the details, but the language and style are not very scientific!

Rewrite the text in formal, impersonal language.

If you have time, you could finish the piece by writing about what probably happened to the plants, and what these results proved.

Our plant experiment

We took three plants. They were all the same kind of plant, and they were all about the same size. David put one plant into a dark cupboard, but we watered it and made sure it had plenty of fresh air. Ravi put the second plant on a nice, bright window–sill. Of course, that one had plenty of fresh air too, but we didn't water it at all. Linzi was in charge of the third plant. She put it on the same window–sill as Ravi's plant, and she gave it just as much water as David's plant. But Linzi put a plastic bag over her plant, so it didn't get any fresh air at all. We all watched the plants to see what would happen.

Hint!

Formal scientific writing is impersonal in style. Use passive verbs to report what happened e.g. 'The plant was put' rather than 'I put the plant'.

2 Read this extract from a journal written by one of Professor Bryte's students.

He has started to learn about using the passive, but he sometimes forgets!

Decide which sentences need changing and rewrite them in the passive.

When the dish was removed from the incubator, it was found to contain a small quantity of blue mould. Professor Bryte examined the mould under a microscope. She found it was of the penicillium type. The culture was divided into several smaller samples of mould. Professor Bryte filled more dishes of nutrient broth. Professor Bryte placed the dishes back into the incubator. She left them for ten days in the warmth. Then she removed them again and looked at the mould cultures. It was found that each small culture had multiplied in size. Professor Bryte had found a way to grow large quantities of penicillium.

Hint!

Here is an easy way to find out if a verb is in the passive:

Find the verb in the sentence. → Find the subject of the sentence. → Does the subject carry out the action of the verb? → Yes → Active verb

↓

No → Does the action happen to the subject? → Yes

↓

Passive verb

How to write

Before starting work, **stop** and **think**.

To help you get ready for writing, consider the following questions:

Who is your **audience**?

What is the **purpose** of your text?

What **text type** will it be? (Be careful! You might need to combine two types.)

How will you **structure** the text?

How will you **sequence** and **link** the text?

What sort of **information** or **ideas** should the text contain?

What sort of **language** will you use?

What star ways can you think of to **impress the marker**?

Now make a quick **plan**.

Make **brief notes** about what information and ideas will go into each main section of the text. You should aim to include:

- an opening section;
- the main section;
- a concluding section.

1   You and your class are on a Media Studies trip to a TV studio. Suddenly a worried-looking director rushes out in front of you, shouting that he needs some more 'extras' for a big scene that they are shooting. He stares straight at you and and a few of your friends, then asks your teacher for permission to 'borrow' you for the rest of the day. What happens next? Write about your acting adventures.

What kind of TV programme do you and your friends find yourselves involved in? A soap opera, a feature film, a documentary, or something else? Are there any famous actors or actresses in the cast?

Remember to include:

- a clear beginning that explains how and why you get involved in the TV programme;

- an outline of the acting job you have to do;

- some interesting things that happen, some people you meet, or some conversations that you have;

- a well-developed ending that refers back to the beginning.

2 As Midge and Jez went up to the door it swung open. They stepped into the room and looked around. "Wow!" breathed Jez, "This is the most amazing place I've ever seen!"

Who are Midge and Jez? Where are they? How did they get there? What is so amazing about the setting? What happens next, and how does the story end? Write about what happens to Midge and Jez.

Decide on a recognisable style to use for your story. You might choose, for example, horror, science fiction or fairytale. Begin by rewriting the introduction appropriately. Then write the rest of the story in your chosen style. Remember to use words and phrases that are right for the style you have chosen.

3 You are a trainee journalist on the staff of *Cool Scene*, a teen magazine specialising in articles about famous personalities in sport or showbusiness. You have been invited to the home of Davie Singer, leading voice of the new hit band *D'lightful*. Your job is to write an article that describes the rock star. You should include descriptions of his clothes and his house as well as giving all the important facts about how the band was formed, what records they have made, etc. The information you need is in the pictures and fact boxes below, but you can make up extra facts if you wish.

The group	
Name of group	D'lightful
No. of members	4 (Davie, Don, Deano, Del)
Group formed	April 2000
Hit records so far	'Always In My Heart' (made it to number 2 in the charts); 'Never Again' (stayed in the top ten for three weeks); 'Don't Say Goodbye' – the group's first number 1 hit

The lead vocalist

Name	Davie Singer
Age	20
Star sign	Aries
Favourite food	pizza
Favourite drink	apple juice
Favourite holiday	sailing/windsurfing

4 You are a sales rep working for Sungold Holidays, and have to write to the Fortunate family to tell them that they have won a holiday. Your letter should tell the family about all the fantastic things to do and see on their holiday island, in the hope that they will accept the prize. (Most of the information you require can be found in the map also sent by the holiday company. You can make up any extra information.)

Remember to tell them:

- how they will get there;

- what the weather will be like;

- what attractions and things to do there are;

- what the hotel will be like;

- any other information that might make the holiday seem extra special.

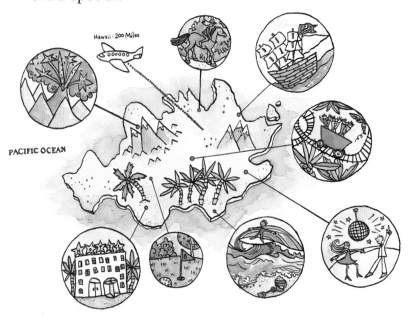

5 You are employed by the local Health Authority to write an important health-education leaflet. The leaflet looks at the benefits of a healthy lifestyle versus the dangers of smoking, drinking and taking drugs. Your job is to try to persuade young adults to think hard and make some sensible choices.

You should look at both sides of the argument, taking into account some or all of the views of the 'unhealthy' group, but showing how and why they are wrong. Make it clear that the 'healthy' group has got the right idea.

Add some ideas of your own if you wish. Remember to make the leaflet interesting enough to grab the attention of young adults.

6　You have been asked to write a short chapter about your favourite sport or game for a book on leisure activities. The book is aimed at general adult readers, and will be published in a country where that sport/game is not played.

You need to include the following information:

- What sort of game is it?
- Why is it popular?
- Where is it played?
- What sort of people play it?
- How is it played?

Your explanation should start from the beginning of the game and follow through each stage, explaining any key rules, right up until the game ends. (Be careful! You should *not* write this out as a set of instructions.)

7　Your school is taking part in an exchange project with a school in another part of the country. Students of your age from the other school will soon be coming to visit your school. Your job is to write a detailed report about your town or village, to give them a clear idea of what it is like. Include detailed facts and information in order to build up a really clear picture of the place and what it is like to live in.

You may wish to include:

- where your town/village is – county, region, other nearby towns;
- anything for which it is well known;
- features of the surrounding countryside – rivers, mountains, lakes, beaches;
- any local customs or traditions;
- key points from the town/village's history;
- fun things to do.

8 Great news! You are going to see a show with your parents and there are two spare tickets. You can offer one ticket to your best friend, but your parents want to offer the other one to your cousin Alex – who you can't stand!

Your job is to write *two* different letters of invitation to the same event, one to your best friend and one to Alex. You can't change any of the facts, but you can present them in a good light or a bad light. Remember you want to persuade Alex to say no and your best friend to say yes! (Be careful – your parents may read Alex's letter, so you mustn't be too rude!)

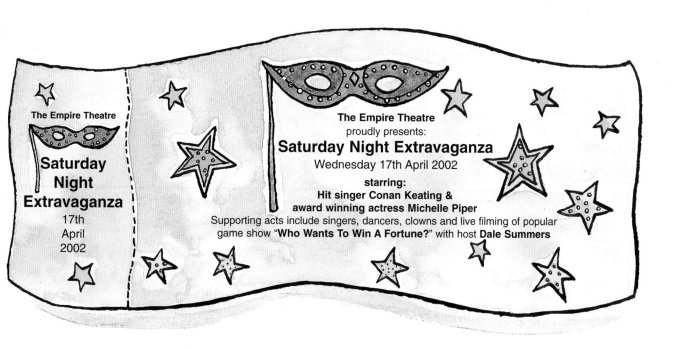

Remember to give each person as much information as you can about the evening (including when and where you will meet, who will be there, etc.).

PUBLISHED BY THE PRESS SYNDICATE OF THE UNIVERSITY OF CAMBRIDGE
The Pitt Building, Trumpington Street, Cambridge, United Kingdom

CAMBRIDGE UNIVERSITY PRESS
The Edinburgh Building, Cambridge CB2 2RU, UK
40 West 20th Street, New York, NY 10011-4211, USA
10 Stamford Road, Oakleigh, VIC 3166, Australia
Ruiz de Alarcón 13, 28014 Madrid, Spain
Dock House, The Waterfront, Cape Town 8001, South Africa

http://www.cambridge.org

© Cambridge University Press 2001

First published 2001
Reprinted 2001

Printed in the United Kingdom at the University Press, Cambridge

Typefaces *Concorde, Frutiger, ITC Kabel*   *System* QuarkXPress®

A catalogue record for this book is available from the British Library

ISBN 0 521 80551 1

Cover design by Traffika Publishing Ltd
Design by Angela Ashton
Picture research by Callie Kendall
Artwork chosen by Heather Richards
Illustrations by James Bartholomew/Heather Richards, Eikon Illustration, Lizzie Finlay/Heather Richards, Sam Hearn/Eastwing, Sally Kindberg, Stephen Lambert/Heather Richards, Ed McLachlan/Folio, Ron Tiner, Thomas Taylor/PFD, Stella Voce/Heather Richards

We are grateful to the following for permission to reproduce text extracts:
'Autumn Gale' by Matt Simpson, from *Read Me: A Poem a Day for the National Year of Reading* (Macmillan Children's Books); *The Not Especially Fascinating Life So Far of J. K. Rowling* © www.okukbooks.com; *Truth or Dare* © Celia Rees, 2000 (Macmillan Children's Books); *Step by Wicked Step* © Anne Fine, 1996, reproduced by permission of Penguin Books Ltd; *The Emerald Conspiracy* by Mark Fowler, reproduced by permission of Usborne Publishing, 83–85 Saffron Hill, London EC1N 8RT. Copyright © Usborne Publishing Ltd; 'The Charge of the Mouse Brigade' by Bernard Stone, from *The Kingfisher Book of Comic Verse* (Kingfisher Books); *South by South East* © 1997 Anthony Horowitz, reproduced by permission of the publisher Walker Books Ltd, London; *The Illustrated Mum* by Jacqueline Wilson, published 1999 by Doubleday, a division of Transworld Publishers. All rights reserved; *Harry Potter and the Prisoner of Azkaban* and *Harry Potter and the Philosopher's Stone* copyright © J. K. Rowling 1997.

We are grateful to the following for permission to reproduce photographs and illustrations:
17a, 25, 50, 52, Rex Features Limited; 17b, 19a, 29a, Lucasfilm Ltd/The Kobal Collection; 18, 22, 26, Mary Evans Picture Library; 19b, 19c, 21a, 21b, The Kobal Collection; 21c, 29b, © David B. Fleetham/www.osf.uk.com; 23 (both), The Stock Market; 37, © Kos Picture Source; 44a, © Howard Hall/www.osf.uk.com; 44b, © Kim Westerskov/www.osf.uk.com; 48a, 48c, © Bubbles/Ian West; 48b, © Bubbles/John Howard; 63a, © G. I. Bernard/www.osf.uk.com; 63b, Tek Image/Science Photo Library; 64, 65, www.shoutpictures.com.

Every effort has been made to trace all copyright holders. If there are any outstanding copyright issues of which we are unaware, please contact Cambridge University Press.